FLOWER PAINTING

First published in the United States of America in 1986 by
Rizzoli International Publications, Inc.
597 Fifth Avenue, New York, N.Y. 10017

Library of Congress Cataloging in Publication Data

Sydney, Clare.
  Flower painting.

  Bibliography: p.
  1. Flowers in art.   2. Painting, Modern—20th century
3. Watercolor painting—20th century.   I. Title.
ND1400.S94   1986   758′.42   85-43478
ISBN 0-8478-0695-2 (pbk.)

Printed in Great Britain by Blantyre Printing
and Binding Company Limited, Glasgow

Fallen Tulips by Elizabeth Blackadder. 1982. Watercolour,
$22\frac{1}{2} \times 31$ in. Collection Michael
Ginesi

FLOWER PAINTING

CLARE SYDNEY

RIZZOLI
NEW YORK

Elizabeth Blackadder 1982

1. Eliot Hodgkin. *Plantain*. 1940. Tempera. Collection Sir Alfred Beit.

It was Cedric Morris's conviction that 'only a modest man can paint a flower'. The remark was made in 1942, in his article, 'Concerning Flower Painting' in *The Studio*, in which he distinguished between the artist who just happens to do a good painting of flowers, and the real flower painter whose love of flowers extends to an intimate understanding of their growth. He particularly admired the way Chinese artists acquired such familiarity with a plant, that they could distil that experience into a single image (Fig. 2); painter and plant are at one in a way that admits no feelings of either superiority or inferiority. The idea relates very closely to our own ecological understanding of continuity and change, and of the interdependence of all matter. Morris himself was outraged at the effect an arrogant misuse of chemicals was having on our environment. But there is another sense in which his sentiment on modesty is particularly pertinent. Every artist who tries to set down his relationship with the physical world in paint, has to accept that the human eye can no longer fully observe the vistas opened up by scientific discoveries. And whether conscious or not of directly acknowledging this challenge, artists in the modern period have attempted as never before to extend their perception of nature.

In the early part of the century, American artists like Charles Sheeler, Joseph Stella and Georgia O'Keeffe dealt with abstract forms of plants and their underlying structures, or were stirred by their colours. 'The terrific zing of a violet vibration', Patrick Heron was enthusing in the early sixties, 'a violent violet flower, with five petals, suspended against the receptive furry green leaves in a greenhouse!' There were some who never ceased to represent the visible world or who, with a sigh of relief, rediscovered it as an acceptable subject for painting in the post-war period. These artists draw on traditional and, increasingly, photographic means to describe their experience of plants and flowers in fresh, ornamental and, often, highly subjective ways. Among those who were brought up on the teachings of modernism, but who have since turned to natural-istic painting, a number have sought to abstract the essence and spirit of flowers in order to seize another kind of truth. As a result, painting in the second half of the twentieth century has displayed a remarkable new diversity in its artistic and emotional response to nature.

Surprisingly though, flower painters have found little to excite them in the use of high-precision scientific equipment. As is well known, botanical draughtsmen rely on the microscope to examine flower parts that are difficult to discern in detail with the casual eye alone. For one reason or another, non-specialists favour the camera, either as a mechanical aid to perception, as a tool to simplify or edit reality, or as a practical means of preserving a perishable flower arrangement. The decorative possibilities of microscopic enlargements, which appealed to the American artist,

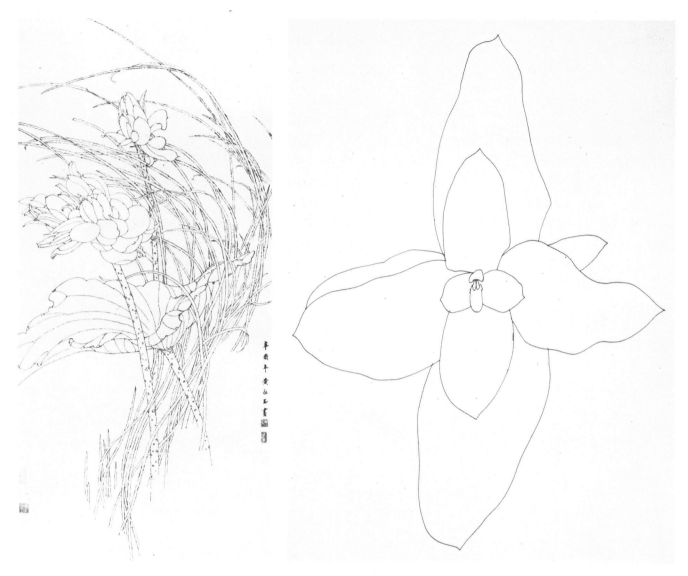

2. Huang Yongyu. *'Baimiao' Lotuses*. Dated *xu you*, 1981. Hanging scroll, Chinese ink on paper, $51\frac{1}{4} \times 25$ in. (130 × 63 cm.) Private collection of the artist, Beijing.

3. Ellsworth Kelly. *Milkweed*. 1969. Ink on paper, 29 × 23 in. (74 × 58 cm.) Private collection.

Arshile Gorky, in the forties have not been pursued. It may be that as artists find new meaning in their relationship with the real world, these hidden structures are simply less exciting because too remote from everyday human experience. When Ellsworth Kelly investigates the same flower as Gorky, peering into the heart of the milkweed, he attempts to capture its essential form with the most economic line possible but he renders a totally recognizable image (Fig. 3). Seemingly, artists prefer to find visual equivalents for what they can see with their own two eyes, and which they can respond to directly. Any further explorations into the mystery of flowers is left to the imagination, and to the artist's immediate engagement with paint and surface.

Cedric Morris's own flower pictures have a striking way of suggesting more than he actually defines with dabs of thick paint (Plate 25). This unusual ability may have had something to do with the almost matey relationship he had with the plants he propagated as well as painted. It was as if artist, gardener and plants were somehow in collusion. One of the friends who shared his passionate interest in the individuality of plants was John Nash (Fig. 4), a neighbouring artist-plantsman in East Anglia. Nash illustrated a number of books on botanical subjects which display his sensitive observation and strong sense of design to good effect. Among them were *Poisonous Plants* (1927), *Plants with Personalities* (1938), a theme he particularly enjoyed working on, *The Curious Gardener* (1932), *The Contemplative Gardener* (1940) and *The Tranquil Gardener* (1958). It

4. John Nash. *Morina longifolia*. 1975. Watercolour, 20¼ × 12 in.
(51 × 30.5 cm.) Private collection.

was in the fifties that he was able to pass on some of his acquired knowledge and pictorial judgement by teaching plant illustration at Flatford Mill Field Centre, and he admitted that 'the distinction between a good and a bad plant drawing is hard to make. If you look at the plant-draughtman's Bible, Wilfred Blunt's *Botanical Illustration*, you will find some illustrations which conform to the need for accuracy combined with the spark of a live drawing, as well as much work which may serve its purpose but gives no feeling of the living subject.'

Blunt's survey traces the history of botanical art from its earliest, often rather crude attempts to compensate in visual language for the inadequacies of verbal description, to the establishment of scientific drawing as an art in its own right. The aims of the art remain as valid today as they were, in the pre-Christian era, to 'the father of botanical illustration', the herbalist, Krateuas, who painted useful plants for purposes of practical identification. Blunt's book stimulated a number of artists, mostly British, when it appeared in Britain in 1950. But, since that date, increased leisure, spent in the garden and in the countryside, both in Britain and the States has brought with it new commissions for artists to illustrate books and magazine articles on plants and gardens. The need to work quickly and in competition with photography, may account for an accomplished air of painterly ease, which, while pleasing, falls far short of the highest standards of scientific accuracy. On the other hand, one of the most distinguished contemporary artists, Margaret Stones (Plate 14), combines great speed of execution with elegance and precision. Technically and artistically, her work compares with the great classic designs of the 18th and 19th centuries. Paul Jones and Raymond Booth create natural settings for their plants and both, in their different ways, enhance a tradition established by Thornton's famous florilegia, *The Temple of Flora*. Paul Jones keeps his atmospheric backgrounds unobtrusively distant, giving dramatic pride of place to the flower, while Raymond Booth allows a close view of plants growing in environments composed from views of his own garden and of the local Yorkshire landscape. In a different mood, Anne Ophelia Dowden (Fig. 5) looks back to Dürer's *Rasenstück* in her detailed scrutiny of a small patch of wild growth, but reaches far beyond him in her ability to impart vitality to the flora and fauna that inhabit it. The aim of these artists is still to record undocumented species as well as to portray familiar flowers afresh, although few, besides Margaret Mee, have had to contend with the difficulties faced by early explorers. Her journeys down the Amazon and into the Brazilian interior have made a unique contribution to botanical research in an area that is fast being encroached upon by urban developers.

Although they may express it rather differently, most botanical draughtsmen concur with Cedric Morris's belief that the secret of producing a true likeness is never to feel superior to their model. Interestingly, it was a view also held by Oskar Kokoschka about human portraiture, and it is remarkable how closely the two genres overlap and converge in their ambitions. In the figure paintings of Jean Hélion and Matthew Smith flesh appears to flower and flowers to

5. Anne Ophelia Dowden. *Spring Flowers: Oxalis, Fragalia, Taraxacum officinale, Glechoma hederacea, Viola, Waldsteinia fragarioides.* 1964. Watercolour, $9\frac{1}{2} \times 19$ in. (24 × 48 cm.) Hunt Institute for Botanical Documentation, Carnegie-Mellon University, Pittsburgh, Penn.

become flesh. Indeed, flower studies are frequently referred to by their authors as 'portraits', and their sitters as more or less restless or as sporting this or that 'personality'. Cedric Morris himself often used laughingly to refer to particularly blowsy or flamboyant plants as 'tarts', and there is something of this wayward ostentation in Edward Burra's flower pieces (Plate 9), or in the particularly audacious way Georgia O'Keeffe's flowers outface us (Plate 22). Artists will continue to derive as much pleasure from applying their interpretative skills to either humans or flowers, but the great advantage for the painter of flowers is that their subjects neither look critically over the shoulder, nor do they, as yet, answer back.

It may well be that contemporary flower artists will, in fact, find themselves answerable to their sitters one day. Joseph Raffael (Plate 21) and Una Woodruff (Plate 6) enter into an almost mystical or magical communion with the spirit of flowers. Their paintings seem to emanate a powerful life force of their own. The overwhelming size of Raffael's flowers and those of Pat Steir (Plate 26) suggest that beneficent nature can be wonderfully strange, but that it may also be dangerous and consuming. While few artists go as far as P. S. Gordon in floral self-portraiture (Plate 5), we may frequently find ourselves asking as we look at the pictures in this book, whose picture is in fact being taken, the flower's or the artist's. In traditional Chinese art, flower painting was a philosophic exercise in self-expression, but there is never any hint of the unease or self-indulgence found in Western expressionist painting. As we feel the strength of Huang Yongyu's '*Baimiao*' *Lotuses* (*baimiao* means 'plain line'), bowing among windblown grasses, we share his vitality and enthusiasm while admiring his restraint (Fig. 2).

The chatty level on which many Western flower lovers relate to their plants, is caught most delightfully in a letter Stanley Spencer once wrote to his friend and patron, Catherine Martineau:

Dear Cash,

   . . . I have just done my first 1955 pot-boiler; a weeny painting of some snowdrops. They were challenging me from my garden and I had to go to them. There was only one small clump but they are fearfully pleased with themselves. You could imagine them discussing it: 'He's come right to where we are coming out now with a camp stool—there's something up; he has tied a jumper round his head, for warmth, I suppose; goodness now a sort of school satchel and out comes a furry sack which opens in front, and now a hot water bottle of all things. He has put that in the sack, and now he has put himself in the sack, and he is painting: I knew there was something about us.'

The letter is typical of the child-like innocence which kept Spencer's responses to nature continually fresh. His sense that plants belong to another and very real world of their own has been shared by many artists, not least by Anne Ophelia Dowden in her illustrations to *The Secret Life of the Flowers* (1964, Fig. 5). But the 'dialogue' Alice Forman (Plate 31) describes herself as engaging with her environment is perhaps most typical of the aesthetic response and private

6. Audrey Flack. *Time to Save*. 1979. Oil over acrylic on canvas, 80 × 64 in. (203 × 163 cm.) Private collection.

7. Lucian Freud. *Buttercups*. 1968. Oil on canvas, 24 × 24 in. (61 × 61 cm.) Private collection. See also colour detail on cover.

exchange which, within changing cultural boundaries, artists have always tried to encourage between themselves, their chosen flowers and the painting surface.

What distinguishes the manner of today's dialogues is their informality, often bordering on the confidential. And even when paintings are intended for public places like Michael Mazur's mural for Massachusetts Institute of Technology (Plate 29) or Robert Zakanitch's large decorative panels (Plate 24), the language itself is private, and meanings only slowly reveal themselves. The typical Dutch flower-piece of the 17th century was grandly conceived and artificially composed of florists' flowers from different seasons. Conventional symbolism was shared. Only rarely were flowers allowed to relax into studied disarray or adopt a simple pose. Audrey Flack pursues this tradition in her Photo-realist 'vanitas', *Time to Save* (Fig. 6) while Paul Wonner (Plate 1) takes up and elaborates the theme in a contemporary idiom. Today, if flowers are 'arranged' at all, they are arranged naturally by the eye and on the paper. More frequently, the artist encourages the flowers to group themselves casually, or simply to stand around in pots. In Lucian Freud's beautiful painting of a simple bunch of buttercups (Fig. 7, and colour detail on front cover), the artist has placed an armful of flowers, probably from the waste ground outside his studio, in the container that came to hand, an old enamel jug, which he stood in a porcelain sink. We derive the same pleasure from this unpretentious gathering as the artist surely found in transforming his paint so magically into golden petals.

Wild flowers and garden favourites never fail to inspire, but much of the revived interest in flower painting seems to have been stimulated by the wider range of plants available—exotic pot plants as well as all sorts and new varieties of cut flowers. Chosen environments, on the other hand, are familiarly domestic—studio, kitchen, living room, dining room—the settings frequently intimate, rarely 'tidied up' for the occasion. Whereas the Impressionists took flower painting out into the fresh air of the countryside, the twentieth-century artist has brought a similar cult of relaxation, sunshine, and fresh air colour and atmosphere to interior flower pictures. David Hockney's crisp drawing of a bunch of asters is so immediate in its conception that, like classic Chinese paintings, it seems to be coloured by ink alone (Fig. 8). And like them, it is convinced of what it wants to say.

What is surprising is that a dialogue persisted at all in the post-war modern era. Until well into the seventies, naturalistic flower painting was considered to be amateur subject matter, an old-fashioned pre-Modernist genre appropriate only for elderly ladies and concierges, certainly not for up-and-coming students hoping to establish themselves in the vanguard of contemporary aesthetics. Of course, independent spirits survived, particularly within what has come to be called 'the alternative tradition', and particularly in garden-loving Britain which has always harboured loyal patrons for serious flower painters like Stanley Spencer, Cedric Morris or Eliot Hodgkin among the older generation, or Raymond Booth among the younger. In America, Morris Louis's *Iris* of 1954 and his *Floral* series are among the beautiful and delicately stained canvases he was producing in the fifties. The evocative *Iris* with its diaphanous and shadowy mauve, blue, pink, yellow, green and brown 'veils', and his brilliant bursts of separately articulated 'petals' were proof that the colours of flowers could still be inspirational. But where Louis's experience was seemingly fragile, the watery pigment enclosing some elusive and universal idea of beauty, the Pop artists of the succeeding generation were concerned with the general and unspecific image of 'the flower' only because it was demonstrably ubiquitous, just another item of twentieth-century urban culture. In the painting of Roy Lichtenstein and Andy Warhol in the States, and of Patrick Caulfield and Richard Hamilton in Britain, the meaning of flowers was reduced to its most crudely sentimental and banal.

This attitude was finally summed up in Richard Hamilton's perverse flower-pieces of the seventies that polarized a vase of flowers and a heap of turds, and reminded us, in the conventional terms of the 'memento mori' that 'life is not all prettiness and fragrance'. Hamilton's sceptical look at the genre of flower painting also posed questions about the way we have raised flower

8. David Hockney. *Flowers in a Glass Jug.* 1975. Pen and ink, 14 × 17 in. (35.5 × 43 cm.) Collection Mr and Mrs H. Feiwel.

pictures to the status of icons, promoted 'the bouquet' to something vaguely heroic, and distributed flowers en masse in catalogues, advertisements and magazines, bearing vacuous sensory messages suggestive of 'perfumed freshness', 'allure', 'romance' and 'glamour'.

The hollow sentimentality of this commercial language of flowers had first been given currency by Roy Lichtenstein. In one of his earliest paintings using advertising imagery, *Black Flowers* of 1961 (Fig. 9), he had already turned the cliché 'flowers are beautiful' on its head by producing an image of extraordinary ugliness. The painting is strongly designed on two planes: the tulips ponderously outlined in black and set against a background of small Benday dots. The result is a tasteless 'machine-produced' image described by one critic as 'the Woolworth's contribution to the art of flower arrangement'. Any suggestion that these 'black' tulips might have emerged from some refined atmosphere of exotic blooms and elegant gardens is at once destroyed by their similarity to cheap plastic imitations.

9. Roy Lichtenstein. *Black Flowers*. 1961. Oil on canvas, 70 × 48 in. (178 × 122 cm.) Collection Walter and Dawn Netsch, Chicago.

Flowers were removed even further from reality in Andy Warhol's 1964 flower panels. Not only were the images crudely drawn, stylized versions of photographic images and thus deliberately second hand, they were painted in lurid colours and arranged as infinite 'repeats'. The largest of them, almost twelve feet square, resembled advertising hoardings both in the way they shrieked out at the passer-by and in their impersonal surfaces. We respond to them simply as spectacular painting, but the image they present of flowers is tired and anything but tempting.

These billboard flowers came along with canned foods and money bills, as just another desirable consumer item in our materialistic society. But what Pop artists left out of consideration, and what Don Nice (Plate 28) has put back into painting, was the fact that flowers were, and continue to be a spiritual resource for many people. Marc Chagall saw God in every bunch of flowers, and his myriad coloured petals produced a shimmer of paint like some angelic apparition. In a post-war society which manages largely without the inspiration of a god, artists have rarely responded in such expressly religious terms.

Eliot Hodgkin's tempera paintings of ruined classical buildings and of London's abandoned sites, include fresh and beautifully detailed studies of wild flowers pushing their way resolutely through the empty ruins (Fig. 1). The concept is a romantic one, but there is no sentimentality in the keenness of Eliot Hodgkin's attention. Instead, there is something reassuring and consoling about this vision of nature as a decoratively healing agent, capable of rehearsing endlessly the earliest processes of creation. Nature, both in its vastness and its minute detail, is seen as life-giving as well as life-enhancing, and many artists and writers have paid tribute to its restorative and therapeutic powers. Indeed, several artists in this book, Marie Angel, Margaret Stones and Raymond Booth (Plates 8, 14 and 15), who have all made flower painting a speciality, were drawn initially to the subject through prolonged illness. Flowers are easy to come by, are of manageable proportions and can be painted almost anywhere. For this reason too, perhaps, artists like Oskar Kokoschka (Plate 27) pursue their interest in flower painting or discover new inspiration as they get older, and as the desire to travel round the world seeking novelty lessens or becomes physically impossible.

Of course, there are others, Francis Bacon for one, who express the heights and depths of human experience in real moments of great beauty and violent ugliness, and who only rarely paint a flower. Bacon said recently, maybe because he felt all too aware of approaching old age, that he found Monet's water lilies 'depressing' because they were 'going to die'. But for the artist who revels in his garden as Monet did, the dying flower is a prelude to new growth. For the real flower painter there is no dead season, only another stage in the natural order of things. Elizabeth Blackadder's tulips bend and unfurl most gracefully (Title page). Petals fall and in their very pattern seem to express the artist's serene contemplation of that order.

I

PAUL WONNER
(American, *b.* 1920)

Metropolitan Flowers (1983)

Acrylic on canvas,
72 × 50 in. (183 × 127 cm.)
Private collection, on loan to The
Boston Museum of Fine Arts

Flowers have gradually become the central theme of Paul Wonner's still lifes. He is drawn to them instinctively and with great affection, despite the fact that he was brought up to consider them unworthy subject matter for a professional artist. He now expresses the inspiration and very positive sense of pleasure he derives from flowers by referring to them in their past as well as in all their current manifestations, from the commercial to the purely aesthetic. Here he quotes the lavish arrangement by the nineteenth-century American artist, Severin Roesen, which adorns the title page of the book *Metropolitan Flowers* (see bibliography). Flower is heaped upon flower in sprawling superabundance. Paul Wonner's much sparer still lifes represent very personal versions of earlier rather formal masterpieces. They give the flowers space and they take themselves less seriously, but like his Dutch models, they are additive. For Paul Wonner's arrangements, contrary to appearance, are never calculated. A witty man, he likes surprise.

Metropolitan Flowers started with a bucket of flowers brought by a friend from the country and then one thing, literally, lead to another. A head of hydrangea was cut, a small painting of a tulip added, then a Japanese plate and a seed packet. The final result is a flower lover's anthology laid out on the floor like an interior landscape garden. The variety of perspective lines ensures that our eyes are not swept away towards a single vanishing point but can scan the panorama from different angles.

Paul Wonner finds much to amuse him as well as to seduce him in the contemplation of flowers. Great game is to be made out of placing some grand or exotic flower in an empty tin can or in a humble bottle, 'the privileged and the unprivileged' side by side, as he puts it.

2

ANNE MARIE TRECHSLIN
(Swiss, *b.* 1927)

Blanc Double de Coubert (1980)

Watercolour over pencil on paper,
$16\frac{1}{2} \times 9\frac{7}{8}$ in. (42 × 25 cm.)
Collection of the artist

This beautiful French rose, raised in 1892, is named after the village of Coubert just south of Paris, where it grows vigorously on sandy soil. Its translucence and its night-time fragrance give it a special place among Anne Marie Trechslin's favourite choice of scented and white flowers—lily of the valley, lilac, rose and camellia. The delicate texture of its cold white petals is achieved without any use of white paint. Instead, many shades of 'gris colorés' are brought into play on warm white paper—palest violet, lilac, green or lemon yellow.

Anne Marie Trechslin is charmed by every variety of wild and cultivated flower but, since 1965, she has made roses her speciality and devoted several of her many illustrated books exclusively to them. Her dedication to cultivating a beauty suggestive of soft fragrance and heady perfumes prompted one of her authors, André Le Roy, to style her 'the Redouté of the twentieth century'. In 1967, the famous French rose growers, H. T. Meilland, conferred a further honour on her by giving her name to a sweet-smelling apricot-pink rose of her own choice. She is the first botanical artist in recent times that the firm has thus celebrated for her truthfulness and artistry. For, if the rose is the much-lauded beauty queen among flowers and all too often crowned with sentimentality and vulgarized into chocolate box 'kitsch', Anne Marie Trechslin's fine rose portraits are distinguished by their honest regard for the singular beauty and personality of each plant.

The same may be said of her equally fine bird pictures. Growing up in the countryside around Paris, her sensitivity to the natural world was awoken early and she remains continuously curious about it. When she explores the form of a new rose, it is almost as though she were discovering the contours of an unfamiliar and slowly unfolding landscape, and she is always conscious of the need to let her own personality vanish into it.

3

ELIOT HODGKIN

(British, *b.* 1905)

April (1951)

Tempera on board,
10¼ × 8¼ in. (26 × 21 cm.)
Private collection

One of a series of 'Twelve Months', the selection for April includes, (clockwise from upper left), the common English daisy, blooms of the double and single *Camellia japonica*, *scilla campanulata* (*Endymion hispanicus*), *Helleborus foetidus*, plum-coloured auricula, the so-called 'pom-pom' daisy, the lady tulip, pink *Primula veris*, japonica or flowering quince and polyanthus, together with horse chestnut, radish, new potatoes and spring onion.

After careful deliberation with gardening friends Eliot Hodgkin designed this charming and precisely observed arrangement to typify the fresh radiant beauty of April. A master of tone and delicately gradated colour harmonies, he has brought into play all the glowing pinks and silvery greens which follow the vivid brilliance of early Spring leaves and yellow flowers. Although no longer a practising Quaker, Eliot Hodgkin is, in the broadest sense, a religious man, moved by a deep sense of unspoken wonder and excitement before the world.

It is not surprising to learn that he drew his first inspiration for finely detailed painting from a page of Illuminated Hours decorated by the Master of Mary of Burgundy. Like this mediaeval miniaturist, Eliot Hodgkin offers us an ordered world in microcosm, in which the crisp petals of the camellia and the delicate silky skin of the new potato are sympathetically related, and rendered with exquisite definition and with equal affection. The emotional charge of his painting, enthused by more than a dash humour, argues against his own insistence that he is simply 'copying' what is in front of him. The medium of egg tempera is, by its nature, slow. It demands minute and repeated touches of pure pigment to achieve the luminous colour and evocative textures that delight in Eliot Hodgkin's work. So, for practical reasons, he choses either longer lasting flowers which hold their shape over several days, or works from careful drawings, but with results that are far from studied. The sheer vitality of his line ensures that nature quickens, and buds burst.

Eliot Hodgkin April 1951

4
PAUL GELL
(British, *b.* 1928)

August Triumphant (1984)

Watercolour on paper,
$39\frac{3}{8} \times 27\frac{1}{2}$ in. (100 × 70 cm.)
Private collection

Like Oriental artists, Paul Gell has always felt in close and easy communion with nature and he has always painted from life, but he only turned his full attention to plants and flowers when he started experimenting further with watercolours in 1978. He now lives in the seclusion of a high-walled garden on the south coast of England where he can walk among plants and observe the delights and caprices of their individual personalities from year to year, day by day, season by season and in every weather. His pictures continually express his admiration for every kind of flower, an affirmation of life best summarized in the introduction to his book, *Flowers from a Painter's Garden* (1983): 'The extraordinary thing for me is how flowers come into being at all—how they survive frost, wet, drought, not to mention the wilful destructiveness of man or beast. This triumph in adversity, the survival of life itself, is what I want most to capture.'

August Triumphant is a virtuoso statement of this intent, in terms both of its brilliance and of its complex juxtapositions of forms and colours. Paul Gell never copies a frozen image. In common with all his pictures, this arrangement grew instinctively under the brush. The artist started with the glorious scarlet gladiolus. His eye then picked out flower after flower from those already cut, and dotted about in vases. His studio is continuously alive with blooms gathered daily from the garden. Jars often stand on a lazy Susan, ready to be swivelled to give different viewpoints, back as well as front, for Paul Gell appreciates the movement of plants and responds to every nuance of change and development that may be occasioned by the vagaries of the weather. And so the character of the painting evolved until the final bouquet was complete: gladioli, belladonna lilies, hybrid lilies, dahlias, zinnias and lavetaria in nonchalent profusion.

Working directly onto the paper, in a manner comparable to traditional Chinese artists, Paul Gell makes bold abstract marks, controlling the subtle gradations of colour and texture with large brushes of transparent watercolour. By this impromptu method of painting he catches the casual attitudes of flowers, nodding and bending this way and that, with striking truthfulness.

August triumphant   Paul Keller 84

5

P. S. GORDON
(American, *b.* 1953)

*Flora, Flora, Where's the Fauna?
Starling under Glass* (1984)

Watercolour and gouache on paper,
52½ × 40¼ in. (133.5 × 103 cm.)
Collection Mrs Glenn C. Janss

This immense floral dance is a romantic self-portrait of a most unusual kind, and is one of P. S. Gordon's most ambitious still-life portraits on a floral theme. Artistically, it offers an elegantly refined pun on the reality of Realism; as an honestly observed summary of a personality through his possessions and acquisitions, the tableau encapsulates P. S. Gordon's own experience of illusion and disillusion with amazing technical virtuosity.

The atmosphere is almost oppressively heady: a massive swathe of glazed chintz in which nestles a bewildering medley of translucent and transparent, sensuous and inert surfaces. Gorgeously coloured flowers sing out of a sultry ground, and indulge in an elaborate game of magical hide-and-seek with what is and what is not. P. S. Gordon is prepared gently to confuse, even mislead us while giving every opportunity to play along with his delightful puzzle. The bizarre title of the painting, *Flora, Flora, Where's the Fauna? Starling under Glass*, so characteristic of his off-beat mid-Western humour, extends a teasing invitation to explore the nostalgic trail of emotive objects: the starling chattering over its stuffed and encased companion, the small vase of bleeding hearts beside an arrangement of spring flowers—red and pink tulips, parrot tulips and anemones—the iron song bird in its trellis looking back over the involved scene. Although large, this painting is intimate in scale, and allows the viewer to become closely engaged in what is, in fact, an optimistic—not too serious—view of the world. P. S. Gordon was brought up in the small country town of Claremore, Oklahoma whose one claim to fame is that it gave birth to the humourist, Will Rogers. His grandmother was a florist, his mother a painter of naturalistic oils. The old family house, full of flowers, paintings and treasured objects, has been a rich source of inspiration for his lovingly painted precisionist watercolours.

6
UNA WOODRUFF
(British, *b.* 1951)

Buddleia (1984)

Watercolour over pencil on paper,
$11\frac{1}{4} \times 14\frac{5}{8}$ in. (28.5 × 37 cm.)
Private collection

One of a series of four: *Hydrangea, Pinks*, and the pendant to *Buddleia, Tiger-Lilies*. The association of butterflies with the buddleia is a commonplace, but Una Woodruff has taken the relationship one stage further in her belief that the stuff of insects and flowers, indeed of all forms of life, is essentially the same. This realization grew from the visionary experiences of a childhood spent in the ancient Welsh border country: maggots and flies emerged mysteriously from fruits, fairy faces haunted hawthorn hedges and spirits danced in trees. And, as she innocently observed, the petals of pressed flowers bore a natural resemblance to butterfly wings. Inspect the buddleia sprays closely and the familiar peacock, tortoiseshell and small copper butterflies are seen to converge, not on mauve flower spikes, but on lively clusters of the common blue. A metamorphosis takes place, literally, in front of our eyes. Is it optical illusion—or is it magic? A hint of playful duplicity appeals to Una Woodruff's sense of humour but, ultimately, she is less concerned with games of artifice for their own sake than with deploying visual metaphor to illuminate life's cyclical change, renewal, and continuity.

Her effects are ingenious and often startling. Wriggling caterpillars take root, blossom as butterflies or dragonflies, and fly away. The conceit of the Butterfly Bush is an archetypal image for just another of the natural coincidences and correspondences that Una Woodruff sees around her. Others, recalling Edward Lear, are more fanciful extravaganzas: cowslips, pussy-willow, catkin, pollyanthus flaunting squawking parrot heads, and croakus, a riot of frogs.

In 1909, the distinguished designer Lewis F. Day maintained that 'knowing retards our flight into Fairyland'. Una Woodruff's crypto-botanical specimens are proof enough that that alternative world exists. It was already evident in her first book, *Inventorum Natura* (1979), a worthy heir to Pliny's *Natural History*, and two years later in *Amarant: the Flora and Fauna of Atlantis*, supposedly by a seventeenth-century amateur, Lady Elizabeth Hurnshaw.

7

JEAN MARIE TOULGOUAT
(French, *b.* 1927)

Bank of Crimson Flowers (1984)

Oil on board,
14½ × 20½ in. (36.8 × 52 cm.)
Private collection

Jean Marie Toulgouat was born in Giverny the year after Claude Monet, who was distantly related by marriage, died. His childhood was spent in the atmosphere of Monet's recent memory and in the presence of his last great canvases. As a boy he was given help with his own painting by his aunt, who was also an Impressionist. Later, following two years at the Art Academy in Nice, and in a bid for independence, Jean Marie Toulgouat decided to train as an architect. He spent six years in practice in Paris, where his talents were eventually employed on landscape architecture and on the creation of beautiful environments, a specialization for which his early years had sensitively prepared him. But his predilection for the countryside and for painting finally drew him back to his roots in Giverny. To some extent, architectural values continued to inform his new work. But gradually abstract structures became more organic. Flowers as well as landscape now inspire his painting.

Jean Marie Toulgouat rarely works directly from nature although his studio overlooks his garden. Rather, as in this highly-charged painting of oriental poppies growing between drifts of cornflowers, he conveys his raw emotional response to what he sees and knows well. He has made many such pictures, some similar in their heightened mood, others quieter and more softly toned, but all brushed in with a spontaneity and controlled fluency akin to Oriental calligraphy. Occasionally the character of a flower he is depicting is so strong that it demands identification. More often individual qualities assume less importance than the pure retinal sensation conveyed by light, colour and movement. In *Bank of Crimson Flowers* the large flimsy petals of the poppy are massed together as if touched by a wayward breeze.

8

MARIE ANGEL
(British, *b.* 1923)

Rabbit's Ears (Stachys lanata)
and Violas (1979)

Watercolour over pencil on paper
$8\frac{5}{8} \times 6\frac{3}{8}$ in (22 × 16.2 cm.)
Collection of the artist

In mediaeval cottage gardens flowers took their place in borders beside herbs and vegetables. Valued as much for their medicinal and culinary properties as for their fragrance and decorative appeal, there was nothing strange about their sharing the same patch with the cabbages and leeks. Just as the cottage gardens themselves were corners of nature claimed for cultivation, so many of the flowers in them—heartsease, cowslip, foxglove, honeysuckle, primrose—were brought in from the wild. Many other plants, now regarded as traditionally English, were in fact imported and naturalized, some as late as the 19th century, and their popular names have probably done as much as their hardy natures to enhance their appeal: batchelor's button, bleeding heart, sweet william and snapdragon. The aptly described rabbit's ears, with its furry white leaves and small pink flowers, is also known as lamb's ears, lamb's tongue and Saviour's flannel. It enjoys a favourite place in every country child's memory, as indeed it does for Marie Angel who spent many months as a young girl confined to bed with a pet rabbit as her only playmate.

Marie Angel's interest in cottage gardens and their flowers began fifty years ago when she moved to Warlingham in Surrey. Here she was charmed as much by the flint and brick cottages as by the old-fashioned planting, which delighted Gertrude Jekyll. In her book, *Cottage Flowers*, the decorative corners evoke the sunny serenity of Helen Allingham's and Beatrix Potter's watercolours. They also remind us of Marie Angel's consummate skill as a decorator of pages. By training a calligrapher and illustrator, she has produced some of her finest work on vellum. Her gifts are those of the miniaturist, and her eye for precise detail is sympathetically suited to the unpretentious character of small flowers in humble settings.

9

EDWARD BURRA
(British, 1905–76)

Flowers (1964–5)

Watercolour and pencil on paper,
30¾ × 40 in. (78 × 103 cm.)
Private collection

These flowers are at once grander, more flagrantly showy and more exotic-looking than in real life. Edward Burra has, as usual, allowed himself strange liberties with their scale, colour and size and, consequently, they are not always easy to identify. This early September bunch came from the herbacious border of his brother-in-law's school near Rye, and includes *Helenium Autumnale* 'Butterpat', a particularly vivid blue hydrangea, which Burra admired, giant montbretia, the white shasta daisy and several varieties of dahlia including the yellow pompon, his favourite, yellow jewel, and a slightly drooping flower head. They were picked by his sister Anne, Lady Ritchie of Dundee, for her mother, and Burra, who loved flowers and gardens, would have picked them again with his eye and drawn them from memory in his studio, possibly much later. It was then that his colourful imagination and his talent for decoration could take flight over the page. Like the human characters in his dramas, Burra puffs up the curves of flowers, caricatures their features and exaggerates their excrescences. There is always a mixture in his work of the stylized and the stylish with what has been artfully observed. An early humorous drawing, done when he was eighteen, shows three girls sprouting creeper covered in flowers and fruit from their mouths, ears and breasts, an early indication of the anthropomorphic possibilities which Burra saw in natural forms and which he would exploit throughout his work. A little later he cut out photographs of flowers, using the seductive forms of the fuschia and pansy to characterize a hand or a face. More typically, the plants, flowers and trees that form part of the Burra scenery, take their mood from the picture itself, and can be made to reflect anything from the sultriness of the opium den, to the disrespectful and disreputable airs of his low-life populace. But it is not until the large still lifes, painted in the fifties and sixties, that opulent bouquets form the centre-pieces of Burra's fantasy world.

10

OTA JANEČEK
(Czech, *b.* 1919)

A Fisherman (1950)

Oil on canvas,
25½ × 36 in. (65 × 92 cm.)
Collection of the artist

Nature, in all its significant forms and mysterious processes, has been a source of inspiration for Ota Janeček's work from his earliest landscapes in the manner of Cézanne to his most recent poetic evocations of natural scenery and events. His contemplation in symbolically abstract terms of bursting poppy seedheads is as typical of his response to the minutiae of natural life as is this more realistically observed bank of wild flowers and grass husks. Ota Janeček enjoys walking in the countryside and fishing in his spare time and his many paintings of grasses draw directly on the experience. The phrase, 'that eternal song of the grass', with which the poet František Hrubín once described Janeček's lyrical variations on this theme, aptly conveys the heightened mood of this painting. The artist appears to be sitting hidden in the thick of a deep tangle of flowering weeds, which still display the moist luxuriance of early summer brilliance. The detailed scrutiny of leaf and stalk structure, familiar in other paintings by Ota Janeček, has been replaced by a fluent, more decorative shorthand in an attempt to catch the rhythmic movement of the grasses against mysterious depths of vegetation.

Ota Janeček's sensibility belongs to the world of Neo-Romanticism. It has points of contact with the cool detachment of Albrecht Dürer, the ecstatic intensity of Goethe's Werther lying in a flowery meadow, at one with the world, and with the magic of Paul Klee. More particularly, it draws together the threads of a Romantic movement in Czechoslovakia which sought lyrical inspiration in nature, and which has discovered one of its most sensitive twentieth-century interpreters and illustrators in Ota Janeček.

I I

PANDORA SELLARS

(British, *b.* 1936)

Paphiopedium spicerianum,
Calathea roseo-picta,
Philodendron panduraforme (1985)

Watercolour over pencil on paper,
20 × 14 in. (50.8 × 35.6 cm.)
British Museum, London

Pandora Sellars and her husband, James, complement each other's interests to an ideal degree. His special enthusiasm is for growing tropical orchids, whose sculptural shapes and habits fascinate her as a botanical artist. This Paphiopedium, in particular, she finds irresistibly strange with its curious jutting lip and flying dorsal petal, 'like a nun's starched cowl', but almost crystalline in its gleaming whiteness. Thus her work combines a unique record of his greenhouse successes with a display of her own unusual talents.

The tight and meticulously accurate technique she has perfected over the last decade rarely highlights a specimen drawing in isolation. Much of her country childhood was taken up with exploring the ancient hedgerows near the Black Mountains in Herefordshire, pressing flowers and charting seasonal changes. Her early habit of noticing how one form of life sidles up to another and depends upon it, how fertile nature both allows and controls a teeming crowd, has coloured her own depiction of the naturally vigorous and dense entanglements to be found in the wild. Her illustrations to 'Flora of Jersey' reflect her admiration for the environmental drawings of Paul A. Roberts, while relying on the skills she acquired as a textile designer to put her strongly conceived three-dimensional vision down on paper. In this spectacular composition featuring the Old World orchid, *Paphiopedium spicerianum*, she evokes the steamy jungly atmosphere that is its habitat, and invites the viewer to negotiate a large pillar of the calathea leaf before letting his eye wander into the dark depths of some primaeval forest of philodendron. The painting is one of her most characteristic in its grasp of natural theatre, its preference for dramatic shapes and an almost Baroque chiaroscuro, and in the remarkably intense and endlessly varied green palette with which she sets off rich purple shades and palest orchid tints.

12

JOAN LAW-SMITH
(Australian, *b.* 1919)

Narcissus pseudonarcissus (1983)

Watercolour over pencil on paper,
12 × 18 in. (30.5 × 45.7 cm.)
Collection Mrs John Wyld

Joan Law-Smith grew up with a large garden and a love of trees, birds and plants, but she only began painting flowers as a 'mature student' when her own children had left home. She developed her gift for confident and immaculate definition under the guidance of Paul Jones but quickly established an independent style which tells of her own quiet and gentle personality, and of her poetic sensitivities. The wild daffodils, primroses, buttercups, forget-me-nots and violets in this beautiful Spring frieze are just some of the old English flowers to be found in the garden she has created in Victoria. She included the frieze in *The Uncommon Garden*, which she wrote and illustrated herself. Trying to capture the beauty and grace of these flowers in free growth is as difficult, Joan Law-Smith says, as attempting to naturalize them in an Australian climate. Most of her subjects are picked and painted indoors but the primroses were, in fact, done lying on her tummy on the garden path! The experience recalled the thrill at first seeing primroses on a visit to Hampshire when she was fourteen. She suddenly became aware that she felt far more in sympathy with the delicate sappy plants of the northern hemisphere than she did with the tough-leaved, rather forbidding appearance of much Australian flora. Her love of their cool and peaceful hues is expressed in an almost constant use of white, pinks, pale yellows, mauves and ice blue and her avoidance of strident reds.

Victoria Sackville-West's writings inspired her to put her own feelings into words. *A Gardener's Diary* (1976), originally written in answer to her daughters' repeated requests for gardening tips, and *Gardens of the Mind*, a personal anthology of verse (1979), are both illustrated by Joan Law-Smith. They reveal her spiritual response to nature, reflected through the trials and delights of the practical working gardener, and through the imaginations of those who, like herself, see the joyful existence of the garden as a metaphor for their own lives.

Flowers were a constant feature of Stanley Spencer's paintings throughout his life. Horse chestnuts covered in candles, magnificent displays of may and wisteria, Madonna lilies and lilies of the field, dandelion clocks and bluebells growing wild among the grass, dead tulips being discarded on the rubbish heap. Flowers were a delight to the senses, and as much a part of his homely interpretation of Paradise on earth as were dustbins and his visionary scenes of Christ's Nativity and Crucifixion taking place in Cookham, the Berkshire village where he lived.

Spencer started painting houses and gardens in 1926 and this, one of his most beautiful in its freshness and detail, was completed just after his 66th birthday, two years before he died. The quality of the paint is thin and dry, a characteristic of his later years, but the composition shows no decline in his powers of perception and dynamic recession. Commissioned by Mr and Mrs Jack Martineau, Spencer worked on the canvas between May and early July, spending an hour or so in their garden each evening after Nursery tea. Mrs Martineau recalls how the artist started by touching in the petalled faces of the pink rock roses in the foreground, adding to the composition as buds opened and new flowers came into season: yellow helianthemum, *Alyssum saxtile*, aubretia, yellow cottage tulips and *Cistus pupureus*. So that by early June he was pencilling in the old English tea roses on the right, and filling in the colour with a child size paint brush. Apparently, Spencer was particularly proud of his 'whites'!

This painting, with its play of warm light across terrace and old brick walls, shows Spencer at his happiest and most sensitive. Still very much a child himself, he enjoyed the security of the Martineaus' family circle and he projected his gratitude for their kindness and friendship onto the tulips, in particular, which had stayed open long enough to allow him to paint them all.

14
MARGARET STONES
(Australian, *b.* 1920)

*Sarracenia alata
(Yellow Pitcher Plant)* (1977)

Watercolour over pencil on paper,
22 × 15 in. (56 × 38 cm.)
Collected north of Robert, Louisiana,
on 30 March and 12 April 1977,
by Clair A. Brown
Collection Louisiana State University,
Baton Rouge

This beautiful portrait of the curious insect-eating pitcher plant highlights Margaret Stones's achievement as the most gifted artist working today in the long tradition of botanical art. Classic in her objectivity, her use of unshaded modelling and the isolation of the plant on white paper, she also reveals a Romantic sensibility in the lyricism she imparts to her drawing, particularly of wild flowers. Her assured talent for precise and intelligent scientific observation combines with an innate sense of design as well as a positive enjoyment of what is typical about each plant: the comic behaviour of crocus flowers, the perkiness of cyclamen or the decorative strangeness of pitcher plants with their irregular knotted tubers and untidy foliage. *Sarracenia alata* grows abundantly on marshland and creates glorious greeny yellow pools of colour in Spring.

Margaret Stones was born in Melbourne and it was here, during a slow recuperation from tuberculosis, that she started painting the flowers beside her bed. It was here too that she made the decision to give up her nursing career and to study botanical drawing in the Herbarium at the Royal Botanic Gardens, Kew. She thinks of herself first and foremost as a draughtsman in watercolour, a craft which she has brought to a highly self-critical degree of perfection in obtaining accurate and spontaneous likenesses of what are often very fugitive species. The sheer amount of information she conveys in her drawings, surpassing the most skilled camerawork, is a measure of their scientific value. Temperamentally, she has always preferred the yielding surface of paper to vellum. It suits the rapid and elegant movements of her pencil, a very hard 2H with a long fine point, and the dextrous fluency of her brushwork in building up a remarkably fresh and intense body of colour.

By 1958, Margaret Stones was already principal contributing artist to Curtis's famous *Botanical Magazine*. Ten years later she was commissioned to prepare 250 watercolour drawings for Winifred Curtis's *Endemic Flora of Tasmania*. This was followed by another major commission to record two hundred species of the natural flora of Louisiana for the State University, a body of work which alone testifies to the outstanding quality of her contribution to botanical art.

15
RAYMOND BOOTH
(British, *b.* 1929)

Rhododendron 'Cowslip' (1983)

Oil on card,
13 × 13⅝ in. (33 × 34.6 cm)
Private collection

Raymond Booth planted this handsome variety of rhododendron some twelve years ago. Its size suited his garden and, with an unerring eye for a striking and picturesque subject, he knew that one day it would make an interesting plant to paint. His garden and greenhouses act as a kind of laboratory in which he can study chosen plants in detail and paint them. 'Unpaintable plants', as he describes them, 'I don't bother with.' The appeal of rhododendron 'cowslip' is its splendour as it lights up the garden with glowing trusses of gentle bell shapes. Creamy white flowers flushed with pink are off-set most attractively by fine firm foliage. The intensity with which Raymond Booth has contemplated the plant in his garden before cutting a spray to work from, is reflected in the precise and technically assured way in which he has rendered it. The hang of the blooms, the delicate intertwining of shapes and colours—blue tit, rhododendron and bluebells—the green vividness of an early morning in May all capture the poetry and atmosphere of that moment. Raymond Booth says that his paintings develop slowly as he works on them, that the settings, which so brilliantly enhance his subjects, are partly imagined, but such is his understanding of plants and his faithfulness to them that the illusion of naturalness is entirely convincing. His paintings never lose the joyful impulse of his first vision.

A naturalist and plantsman of international distinction, Raymond Booth was born in Yorkshire where he still lives. Most of the plants, animals and birds that fill his pictures come from his own garden of rare specimens or were seen in the hills, woods and valleys round his home. The continuity of that experience is contained in a remarkable winter diary of 'anything and everything I see as I ramble around the local countryside between the beginning of winter in December, to the full establishment of spring. Nothing is too trivial to include!'

16

SOPHIE GRANDVAL
(French, *b.* 1936)

Dandelions (1977?)

Mixed media: oil on canvas with feathers,
$13\frac{1}{2} \times 9\frac{1}{2}$ in. (34.3 × 24 cm.)
Private collection

The modest beauty of flowers growing in their natural state stirs feelings of elation that the awesomeness of mountains or the majesty of forests fail to do. It is something about their diminutive perfection, and their affinity with the earth which brings us comfortingly close to the source of life and to our own beginnings. In this sense Sophie Grandval's picture of dandelions is unquestionably a product of the Romantic imagination. But its stylized pattern-making and lack of perspective suggest a vision that is at once more innocent and less sentimental. It recalls the Virgin's enclosed garden, with its carpet of flowers untouchable by evil, French sixteenth-century tapestries delightfully strewn with a thousand flowers, or the naturalistic designs on Oriental rugs. Her experience is transcendental, but her magical encounters with nature are real and full of wide-eyed wonder.

Sophie Grandval is entirely self-taught. Her Masters were the flowers, she insists, flowers and a magnifying glass, which she acquired when she was twenty. Her earlier flower pictures displayed single showy blooms, arranged geometrically or decorating a tarot hand. But a visit to South West England, to Bath, at the beginning of the seventies opened her eyes to another dimension. She came for three months and stayed for seven years, utterly entranced by the verdant character of the English countryside. For the first time she began to see flowers as living, rooted plants, and to paint them, lovingly detailed, with their leaves and stalks. Here the dandelion grows for ever upwards, into and out of the picture. And, as her magnifying glass lights on its different aspects, it is transformed from a tight bud, which slowly opens into a gloriously radiant sun, to the decorative clock from which seeds fly through the air like miniature parachutes. The life of the whole field is gathered into this rich golden fantasy—field forget-me-nots, wild parsnip, feathers, several of which are real feathers incorporated into the composition, a butterfly and a bird's egg 'because they appear and ask to be put in'. All flowers and natural forms are shaped after the same idea and by the same Creator, she believes. They speak to her of angels, guardians of the beauty and health of the world.

17
ANTHONY GREEN
(British, *b.* 1939)

*The Flower Arranger/
Early Summer* (1982)

Oil on board,
67½ × 67½ in. (171.5 × 171.5 cm.)
Collection Juda-Rowan Gallery

Nasturtiums and roses are as much a part of the day to day chronicle of Anthony Green's life as are carpets, bikes, beds and bathrooms. But, from a very early age, flowers have always awoken particularly strong associative memories. Sweet peas round his aunt's wartime air raid shelter, geraniums in the London window box, brilliant beds of zinnias in the garden of his French relatives, daisies dotting the grass at his country cottage, Mole End.

Anthony Green made twenty-five paintings chronicling his Cambridgeshire garden and this one, a cornucopia of cultivated and wild flowers, best celebrates the artist's Christian belief in growth and plenitude. The scene evokes to perfection the peaceful late afternoon of a glowing English summer. Shadows are just beginning to finger their way through the grass but the day still stretches clearly into the depths of the picture and up into an infinite golden firmament. Like all Anthony Green's pictures, this one too is autobiographical. The artist sits centrally, admiring his arrangement of honeysuckle, cultivated cornflowers, daisies and cow parsley, stuffed into a fat pot. He is intrigued by the curiously sensual forms of the honeysuckle, and takes pleasure in erotic thoughts.

The richness of detail evinces Anthony Green's skilled pursuit of each plant's idiosyncrasies with very precise brushwork. He delights primarily in the colours of flowers, stripping off much of 'the offending foliage' before making his arrangement. For this reason too, he hates to cut the daisies that decorate the lawn, and has further indulged his enjoyment of them by filling the frame in their glorious celebration.

Anthony Green conceives the enclosed garden both pictorially and intellectually, as an outside room, safely within the human preserve. In the context, cut flowers suggest that we too are living on borrowed time. But, with the knowledge of an eternal Eden, the mood is entirely joyful.

18
PAUL JONES
(Australian, *b.* 1921)

Nymphaea capensis—blue water-lily

Acrylic over pencil on paper,
26 × 18in. (66 × 45.7 cm.)
Private collection

Among the flowers and plants that decorate Paul Jones's home above Sydney harbour is a cabinet displaying his remarkable collection of shells, beautifully arranged in subtle gradations of colour. It speaks serenely of his unceasing wonder at the natural world, at its riches and surprises. His paintings of flowers, on the other hand, are often suffused with unusually strong emotion. Scale and colour are boldly dramatic. His plants appear to be larger than life, the hues of flowers and foliage unbelievably vivid, their presence more solidly tangible and persuasive than in reality. Even the dewy freshness, which is a hallmark of Paul Jones's work, gleams on his leaves like cabochon diamonds. Yet the hyperboles of praise he lavishes on a plant like this handsome and sweet-smelling water-lily are controlled by a meticulous and tender attention to particulars. Each portrait tells of a lengthy, searching involvement with the flower from his many and detailed working sketches to a smoothly perfected likeness.

His career has been one of painstaking dedication to achieving this perfection. As the war years spent painting camouflage drew to their close, Paul Jones made a delicate study of flowers arranged in a posy. It caught the appraising eye of the camellia expert Professor E. G. Waterhouse, who fostered his talent and encouraged him with commissions to illustrate *Camellia Quest* (1947) and *Camellia Trail* (1952). These two books won him international acclaim and another patron passionately devoted to camellias, Beryl Leslie Urquhart. Her two-volume luxury edition, *The Camellia*, was subsequently published with his plates in 1956 and 1960. The unrivalled 'grandeur' which Professor Waterhouse so admired in Paul Jones's paintings of camellias was imparted with comparable virtuosity to a variety of flowers from all over the world that he selected and painted for *Flora Superba* (1971) and *Flora Magnifica* (1976). *Nymphaea capensis* was Plate v in the former volume. This tropical water-lily, now extinct in the Cape, is naturalized in many Queensland rivers, and Paul Jones presents it in its most striking aspect, a twilight vision of blue rising out of the dark water. Both books are distinguished by their romantically rendered backgrounds, some of which are suggestive of a natural habitat, others, sprayed on in subdued tones, create an atmospheric mood entirely the artist's own.

19

LI KUCHAN
(*b.* Li Ying, Chinese, 1898–1983)

Lotuses

(dated *ding you*, 1957, Spring)

Chinese ink and colour on paper,
64 × 33½ in. (162.5 × 85.1 cm.)
Collection Lucy Lim, on loan to The
Brooklyn Museum, New York

'When we see the lotus, we must study this plant. It does not branch or twine. Even though it grows out of mud, it is unstained. Though it comes out of dirty water, it transcends.' The words Li Kuchan inscribed on one of his lotus paintings might equally well apply to this delicate and sensitively drawn evocation of the same plant. The glorious flowers seem to be borne up on an early morning mist of leaves, one pure white bud stretching up to the light. Li Kuchan trained his eye and his hand to seize the poetry of such transient moments by constant sketching. When he was teaching at Hangzhou Academy he was said to hide among the reeds by the lakeside in order to register the movements of lotus plants and birds at dawn and at dusk. First-hand observations and remembered sensations would later merge in a highly personal recreation, not of reality itself but of its vital image in his mind.

Since early childhood Li Kuchan had found both joy and consolation in nature, and in the sketches he attempted to make of it. Born of a poor peasant family, he suffered many hardships in order to gain a formal education at the National Academy of Fine Arts in Peking, and he was fortunate in attracting the support of two famous artists, Xu Beihong and the traditional Master, Qi Baishi. After graduating in 1925, he too became a teacher, venerated into old age. This monumental masterpiece, dated 1957, is a precious survival from a period of socialist upheaval in which many works of art were destroyed by the Gang of Four, and in which traditional painting itself was banned during the decade of Cultural Revolution, 1966–76.

During his traditional training Li Kuchan felt most closely in sympathy with the School of *xie-yi hua*, or 'idea' painting. But he combined the ideals of Chinese abstraction and spontaneous expression with what he had learnt of Western painting from his Masters, among them Xu Beihong, who had studied in Paris. Li Kuchan's loose and sketchy manner and his arbitrary use of colour also suggests the influence of Li Shan, a member of the 'Yangzhou Eccentrics' who introduced an unconventional approach to painting in the eighteenth century. Like Li Shan and later followers of the group, Li Kuchan frequently depicts the leaves of plants in blue or bluish grey. Dabbing his colour on with a damp rag, he creates the highly-praised effect of atmospheric 'blandness', which accords perfectly with the time of day, and which also provides a gentle foil to the vigorous clarity of his calligraphic line.

20

RENÉ MAGRITTE
(Belgian, 1898–1967)

Le Tombeau des Lutteurs
(The Tomb of the Wrestlers)
(1960, dated *1944*)

Oil on canvas,
35 × 46⅛ in. (89 × 117.2 cm.)
Collection Harry Torczyner, New York

René Magritte's wife, Georgette, was proud of her garden, and it is conceivable that Magritte modelled this glowing red rose on one of those perfect specimens illustrated in horticultural catalogues. If so, he would surely have intended us to recognize the allusion. After all, most of us build our ideals of beauty on just such sources. But, equally, 'rose is a rose is a rose is a rose', as Gertrude Stein said. Its source is inconsequential when painted as superbly as Magritte always painted his roses, although nowhere to such exquisite and startling effect. Here it fills our minds and senses as mysteriously as it fills one end of the room with its voluptuous and enigmatic presence and, as one imagines, its pervasive perfume. Magritte has taken the most banal of all sentimental images and endowed it with a new and extraordinary existence.

The rose was a recurrent theme in his work, corresponding to ideas of beauty, love, dreams, passionate desires—and of cruelty. Perhaps the monotony of painting cabbage roses on wallpaper when a young man gave particular edge to his imagination. Whatever the case, this late painting takes on unexpected resonances when viewed in the light of Harry Torczyner's unpublished essay, 'The origins of René Magritte's *Le Tombeau des Lutteurs*' (1985).

Torczyner, Magritte's friend and patron, had just visited the Soviet Union. On hearing that he had not come across any 'Tachist' painters— Magritte's label for the Abstract Expressionists—Magritte remarked: 'They paint white on white, and they believe that this is an achievement.' Harry Torczyner saw Surrealist possibilities in the idea and responded with the challenge: 'from time to time you have filled a room with a green apple, which puts one's teeth on edge. Why don't you paint for me a white rose in a white room, and a window with a view of a snow landscape?' The artist accepted the idea but two months later he was already hinting, in correspondence with Harry Torczyner, of a revolutionary change of colour. Magritte was preparing his patron for a 'leftist arrival'. The provocative title, he explained to another acquaintance, was taken from a book by a French symbolist writer, *Les Ompedailles ou Le Tombeau des Lutteurs*, which he had read as a boy: 'I felt the title fits the idea of a huge red rose filling the space of a room.'

With a sly dig at the 'blindness' of professionals in the art world, Magritte suggested that his work might even be misinterpreted as an abstract or 'Tachist' work, and that its sensational colour would undoubtedly help to draw attention to itself in this context. By dating the work to 1944, during his 'Renoir period', he mischievously set out to confuse the professionals even further.

21
JOSEPH RAFFAEL
(American, *b.* 1933)

Orchid and Shining Spring (1982)

Watercolour and pastel over pencil on
paper,
41½ × 89¾ in. (105.4 × 228 cm.)
The Mann Collection, Highland Park,
Illinois

Joseph Raffael noticed these large hybrid orchids, *Laelia-cattleya*, on a trip to Florida and photographed them. But the aggrandized image he has created, is about more than paying homage to a dazzlingly beautiful flower with its large trumpeting lips and heavy spiced scent. It is about more than simply stunning us by its size into feelings of admiration or respect. It expresses the artist's private attempt to see beyond the facts that define appearance and, by looking more closely at the flower, to penetrate to the mysterious principle of life itself.

The almost hallucinatory process by which Joseph Raffael paints, allowing limpid pools of watercolour to find their own slow-drying forms, is part of this search. The enlarged image projected on his screen provides no more than a referential structure from which, within a pencil tracing, he is free to lose himself actively in improvised play with colours and shapes. The background creates a wonderfully dusky shroud from which this gleaming flower emerges. Brilliant strokes of pastel, which thread through veins and along ruffed edges, evoke the animate night spirit that seems to haunt this ancient and silent plant.

Joseph Raffael has described how, when he moved to the Californian redwoods, the encompassing presence of nature filled him both with awe and with a sense of liberation. He began to devote himself to intimate portraits of water- and wildlife and of romantically isolated flowerheads—water lilies, roses, orchids and irises. Later he pictured the luxuriant jewelled masses blooming in the Luxembourg Gardens in Paris. From all of these experiences he derives peace, inspiration and purpose, and his paintings, particularly those of orchids, celebrate the rites of a universal spiritism, which, he believes, unite mankind and the natural world.

22
GEORGIA O'KEEFFE
(American, *b.* 1887)

Red Poppy (1927)

Oil on canvas,
$7\frac{1}{4} \times 9$ in. (18.4 × 22.8 cm.)
Private collection

'I know I cannot paint a flower, but maybe in terms of paint and color I can convey my experience of the flower or the experience that makes the flower significant to me at that particular time.' Georgia O'Keeffe began to interpret her personal experience of flowers on a magnified scale in 1924 when she became aware of the huge skyscrapers that were going up almost overnight in New York. She realized that, in such a context, no audience was going to have eyes or time to look at things as small as flowers painted by an unknown artist unless it could be startled into noticing what she had to say about them. At the same time her concentrated scrutiny of natural details reflected the concerns of contemporary photographers, and was to some extent influenced by them, notably still lifes like Edward Steichen's lotuses. But Georgia O'Keeffe's aggrandized designs, her manner of boldly confronting the flower face and provocatively filling the frame with it, together with her technical precision, transcended the mechanical means of the camera.

Her naturalism is always simplified, rythmically stylized, never literal; it encapsulates her own vision of a flower like the poppy with its billowing tissue-like petals, its dark blotches and mysterious centre. The visual, sensuous excitement of her painting has suggested certain sexual overtones, particularly in her paintings of the lily, orchid and Jack-in-the-Pulpit with their large protruding stamens or clubs. But Georgia O'Keeffe has never countenanced such interpretations. In her 1976 book, she captioned an orchid with the comment: 'You hung all your associations with flowers on my flower and you write about my flower as if I think and see what you think and see of the flower—I don't.'

23
ROBERT KULICKE
(American, *b.* 1924)

Anemones in a Sung Vase (1984)

Oil on ragboard,
9¼ × 8¼ in. (23.5 × 21 cm.)
Private collection

The eye-catching simplicity of Robert Kulicke's still lifes is one of their lasting charms. Nothing distracts our attention from the single image of a small vase of flowers, or of a piece or group of fruit, offered without airs for our private delectation. Here a quartet of anemones has been quietly disciplined, unruly stems contained within the strong form of a Sung vase, their heads propped around its lip. The painting preserves a short-lived moment of perfection. Half an hour or so later, and we can imagine these curious, restive flowers turning like animals to seek the light. The lush fluency of Robert Kulicke's economic brushwork catches the still serenity of the moment with appealing ease. Or so it seems.

The apparent effortlessness of Robert Kulicke's work belies the care devoted to achieving this effect; up to an hour may be spent setting up the composition, several days painting the same still life again and again, perhaps fourteen or fifteen times, in the hope of coming closer to his ideal of aesthetic harmony and beauty. The subject is immaterial, although Robert Kulicke says he has grown to love flowers. But real flowers make restless models and these anemones are, in fact, of silk. Their qualities provide decorative points of departure for exploring and perfecting, as he says, 'a small piece of intimate pictorial order that I unqualifiedly agree with'. Shape, colour, arrangement must be right in an absolute sense.

On a more intimate level, everything is also felt to be right in a human sense. The painting is hand-size, an icon of perfection for our sensual delight and visual satisfaction. The Sung-style vase is hand-made, potted by Robert Kulicke himself, a reminder that he is a master-craftsman—frame-maker, carver, jeweller and potter—as well as a master of the craft of classical painting. In 1955 he was asked to frame three hundred still lifes by Giorgio Morandi and his long contemplation of an artist he felt temperamentally in tune with, inspired the change we now admire in his own painting.

24
ROBERT ZAKANITCH
(American, *b.* 1935)

Swingers (1981)

Acrylic on canvas,
85 × 79 in. (216 × 200.5 cm.)
Robert Miller Gallery, New York

Robert Zakanitch grew up among flowers, the flowers in his garden and the bright simple shapes which his mother used to embroider into her Czechoslovakian needlework. He still enjoys doing embroidery himself, revelling in the raw stylized effects he can achieve with decorative threads and stitches. During his summer holidays he paints in watercolour, pursuing the delicate and complex forms of flowers in growth on Long Island. In his large architectural pieces he blends his talent for painterly textures and pattern making on the one hand, with an inquisitive interest in organic shapes on the other and, if he uses nature rather apologetically for his own richly decorative ends, he does so with an affectionate and humorous eye on its playfulness.

Take the exotic orchids which inspired *Swingers*, for example. The sinewy curling forms of their petals, exaggerated and brought into movement on a red ground, gave off a hot jungle atmosphere which reminded him of swinging spider monkeys, as well as of improvised jazz rhythms. Many of his carefully composed titles, *Witch Doctor*, *Night Peepers* or *Morning Vanities*, reflect his belief that all energy derives from the same natural source, that in a sense we are all of the same primordial stuff as flowers. Certainly the colours and characteristics of each of his flower abstracts are closely related to Robert Zakanitch's own moods but his concerns as an artist are, initially, formal and objective. The four years that he spent studying the science of colour have made him master over our psychological responses to which the dramatic beauty of flowers in our surroundings contributes in no small measure.

25

CEDRIC MORRIS, 9th Baronet
(British, 1889–1982)

Heralding (1959)

Oil on canvas,
39 × 29 in. (99 × 73.5 cm.)
Private collection

Clockwise from the top, the flowers represented are: *Alium stipitatum*; *Alium siculum*; orico-cyclus iris from Asia Minor; *Iris latifolia* or English iris; *Alium stipitatum*; yellow *Plicata*—one of Cedric Morris's own seedlings; *Iris tectorum*, an iris of which Morris was particularly fond and of which he grew a very rare white form; *Iris japonica*, Ledger's variety; *Iris innominata*; *Alium stipitatum*; English iris; tall bearded iris—Morris was especially pleased with these irises, which he bred himself.

This overture to summer may have celebrated a particularly successful year in Cedric Morris's garden. Certainly he records a selection of the season's flowers with painterly delight as well as with an unostentatious pride in the blossoming personalities of each species. Of all the plants he propagated and whose manners he knew intimately, the iris was, perhaps, his favourite and he described 'the elegance, pride and delicacy of irises', as he perceived them, almost in human terms, to rich and texturally decorative effect.

The highly personal combination of luxuriant colours in *Heralding* is characteristic of Cedric Morris's work of the late fifties and sixties, before it assumed a paler subtlety and beauty. His palette of blues, mauves, acid greens and yellows, plays off the sensual fullness of earliest June flowers, against the misty landscape of the River Brett. The Brett could be seen clearly from his studio window, winding its course through the meadows outside the remarkable art school, which he and his partner, Arthur Lett-Haines, opened in 1937 at Benton End in Hadleigh, Suffolk.

His garden, to which he devoted himself equally until the end of his life, became even more celebrated than the East Anglian School of Painting and Drawing. It attracted many overseas visitors, local parties of gardening enthusiasts, botanists like Nigel Scott, and botanical draughtsmen, like his friend John Nash and the young Mary Grierson as well as British horticultural specialists with whom he exchanged plants, among them Vita Sackville-West, C. H. Grey, John Aldridge, Eliot Hodgkin and Beth Chatto, who in the fifties was just embarking on her career. They came to admire the rare and exotic plants Morris collected on his expeditions to the Mediterranean and elsewhere, as well as the magnificent annual displays of irises. Many of these were newly-created varieties, all hand-pollinated by Morris, which he titled with the prefix 'Benton'. A delicate mauve iris, 'Benton Cordelia', won him the British Iris Society's Silver Medal, just four years after he had received the Foster Memorial Plaque, the Society's highest accolade for individual contributions to the genus *Iris*.

26
PAT STEIR
(American, *b.* 1940)

Nederland Landschaft
(1982)

Oil on canvas in four parts,
$31\frac{3}{4} \times 95$ in. (80.1 × 241 cm.)
The Rivendell Collection

Tulipomania swept Northern Europe into a frenzy of greedy excitement and business transaction in the late sixteenth century. Since that time the flower, with its many and variegated colours, its simple or exotic forms, has been a favourite subject for artists. Yet no-one has made this monstrous craze so pictorially provocative as Pat Steir. Her giant prize tulip cups, sensuously described under a night sky in hues of ravishing nuance, loom seductively into view in ever greater close up, until their great scarlet petals swamp the frame and bemuse our curious eyes.

Pat Steir is not a flower painter but the flower—rose, iris, carnation, tulip—has been a recurrent motif in her work. She started painting their blooms, not for sentimental reasons, but because she admired the possibilities their strong forms offered her as an artist. 'In the flower paintings', she explained, 'I first made a painting of a flower and enlarged it until it became a landscape or an abstraction or a universe. Abstraction and figuration are different ways to inspect the same thing—an image and its meaning, or a mark and how it can seem to become an image, when it is really just a mark.'

A number of Pat Steir's paintings are, in fact, titled 'landscape' and a realistic reading of *Nederland Landschaft* might suggest the vast tulip fields of Holland. In other flower portraits she seems to be offering a botanical exploration of their habit and reproductive organs, but as the image focuses on the flower's interior a myriad petals of carnation, chrysanthemum or cherry blossom explode out of all recognition in a flurry of expressionistic brush strokes. Pat Steir acknowledges her debt to flower artists of the past; their flowers, like her own, are made of paint and the weight of meaning or beauty we attach to them is finally determined by a notion as transitory as that of beauty itself, style.

27

OSKAR KOKOSCHKA
(Austrian, 1886–1975)

Flowers (1972)

Watercolour on paper,
27½ × 20½ in. (70 × 52 cm.)
Private collection

Oskar Kokoschka called flower paintings like this one his 'five finger exercises'. The remark was not meant to imply that he took them any less seriously than other forms of painting. Rather that he cherished the manual dexterity needed to put down directly and spontaneously what his eye saw. Kokoschka never worked with a preliminary pencil design. He liked the immediacy of paint, and his brush would move rapidly about the page allowing a stem to shoot up in one direction, a flower to erupt in another or a single bold red to engage our senses. His colour was always immensely fresh and vibrant, avoiding at all costs what he termed the 'stale salad' look. To Northern eyes it was almost vivid in its harmonies. Brilliant reds, pinks, blues and yellows seem to float in the air, and catch in his abundant use of white paper, the evanescent moisture of the garden.

Kokoschka emigrated to Britain in 1938. He had already formed a particular affection for London and its river, and it was here, between 1939 and 1947, that he began to interest himself more and more in watercolour, completing a large number of flower portraits—roses, irises, lupins, pansies and lilac among them. The iris and rose were two of his favourite flowers and when he returned to watercolour painting again in the fifties, these flowers reappeared in many variations beside whatever novelties his wife, Olda, could find in the market for him.

In 1953 Kokoschka left Britain, where he had taken up citizenship in 1947, and moved to Villeneuve on the Lake of Geneva. The house, modest in size, is set immediately above the shore road, surrounded by trees and shrubs. The main features of the garden are a lawn, carefully tended in the English fashion, and a parterre of flowers. It proved a new source of inspiration and Kokoschka, always an early riser, would be out in the garden among the flowers at seven to see what progress had been made. This assortment of scabious, dog daisy, dahlia and rose, painted when he was 86, shows that he had lost none of his fluency. They are a tribute to his intention never to copy nature but to go out and meet it, and to enable us to meet it too.

28
DON NICE
(American, *b.* 1932)

Alaska Totem : Walker Cove
(1982)

Oil on linen, and watercolour on paper,
108 × 72 in. (274 × 183 cm.)
Private collection

In mid-July 1982 Don Nice was invited by the Natural Resources Defence Council to join a party of interested observers on a boat journey to the fjords of Alaska. It was one of many expeditions he has made in avoidance of highway routes, including extended sailing trips down the Hudson River from his home. In a sense he feels himself an explorer, tracking the footsteps of earlier adventurers and painters, in search of America's greatest undiscovered resource, her wealth of unspoilt natural beauty. England possesses her monumental cathedrals and her neat domestic hedgerows; America has the permanent grandeur of her mountains, her wilderness and wild life, nature in the raw outside everybody's backdoor. These magnificent visual resources are also spiritual resources, in whose celebration Don Nice erects his public altarpieces.

Don Nice has made many paintings in the spirit of *Alaska Totem : Walker Cove*. All of them offer allegories of plenitude in which the abundance of nature—here, flourishing forest, clear water, a myriad wild flowers and reigning eagle, of which hundreds survive undisturbed in North West Alaska—surmounts a predella displaying the popular idea of life's pleasures and necessities—the walking boots, the water bottle, the bunch of wild flowers. Like Renaissance image-makers before him, he translates his sense of the sublime into language that everyone can understand, using the popular imagery of contemporary advertising icons.

As on previous excursions, Don Nice kept a thick watercolour sketchbook filled with his immediate observations of the flora and fauna of Alaska. Ten different species have been intertwined in the composition of this charmingly ornamental surround—Alaska violet, frigid shooting star, Arctic forget-me-not, Alp lily, ground dogwood, pale laurel, heath, rhododendron, buttercups and fireweed. Don Nice's painterly description of each plant in fresh glowing colours offers a suggestive and enticing reminder of the lushness of wild growth that can be experienced in this area of North America.

29
MICHAEL MAZUR
(American, *b.* 1935)

Wakeby Night Study II (1983)

Pastel over monotype,
$47\frac{1}{2} \times 62\frac{3}{4}$ in. (120.5 × 159.5 cm.)
Barbara Mathes Gallery, New York

This is a study for *Wakeby Day/Wakeby Night*, two monumental monotype triptychs commissioned by Massachusetts Institute of Technology for the curved living room wall of a new dormitory. The romantic vision of a moonlit summer night on the bank of Wakeby Lake on Cape Cod was, in fact, composed in the winter. For Michael Mazur's landscapes are fashioned as much by memory and imagination as by direct observation, and the flowers that fill them, never directly representational, are charged with poetic symbolism. In fact, visitors to Michael Mazur's country house are frequently disappointed by the absence of plants at this spot in the garden. The flowers have been transplanted from elsewhere to form a menacing barrier of rampant vegetation, through which we glimpse dark and mysterious spaces beyond and, on the far left, a dazzling reminder of day. The picture is, thus, a projection of the artist's dreams and desires rather than a transcription of reality. Images and after-images are caught in an emotive blend of dark inks, rolled over the plate or painted on in thinned washes, and brilliant pastel colours. The conjunction accords well with the strange indeterminate beauty of the scene and with the artist's search for the truth of his own response to nature.

Michael Mazur started looking more closely at nature in the seventies when he made the decision to move from the polluted atmosphere of New York City to Cambridge, Massachussetts. Since then, flowers have become a figurative device for meditating on the strength and fragility of nature, its growth and decay. In *Wakeby Night*, the sunflowers with their drooping heads adopt a mournful air, recalling both the fading flowers of Charles Burchfield and the myth of Klytie who, according to Ovid, was unrequited in her love for the Sungod. She wastes away and turns into a sunflower, destined vainly to search the sky for her lover. In her forlorn presence the provocative spears of crimson gladioli in the foreground take on a dramatic flame-like quality. Michael Mazur is intrigued by the expressive forms displayed by flowers. The sunflower, cyclamen and calla lily have already appeared in his illustrations to *Les Fleurs du Mal* (1982), where he uses them to embody a similar sense of loss and to reflect on the reality of the human condition expressed in Baudelaire's poems.

30
NELL BLAINE
(American, *b.* 1922)

*Zinnias and Asters in
Fall Bouquet* (1983)

Oil on canvas,
18 × 20 in. (45.7 × 50.8 cm.)
Collection Senator and
Mrs John D. Rockefeller IV

Nell Blaine has established a reputation for handsome and resplendent flower-pieces. Among them are bouquets like this one, more modest in their ambitions. Deceptively simple, they apparently aspire to do no more than present us with a fresh likeness of their subject as the artist ponders some of the autumn splendours of her Gloucester garden. But we deceive ourselves if we read the casualness of her arrangement as anything less than carefully considered. Nell Blaine spends nearly half the year at her Massachusetts cottage where she judiciously selects her flowers for their affinities of shape and, more importantly, of colour. The relationship and balance of these colour values is the key to their exhilarating effect, and it is a mark of the significance Nell Blaine attaches to this aspect of her work that she keeps such careful records in her Journal. Thus for 4 October she noted that this was the second oil done from the same bouquet, and that it comprised the following flowers: lavender and cerise asters, yellow and red canna lilies, salmon-coloured zinnias, orange and red marigolds, pink and deep pink cosmos. Nell Blaine harmonizes them with an assured touch. She is a master at orchestrating primary colours with all their intermediate hues, and restraining them on a cool grey ground. Trembling pinks are never overwhelmed by their more strident neighbours.

In her early years Nell Blaine was a strong admirer of Mondrian and, indeed, the pulse of a painting like *Broadway Boogie-Woogie* echoes distantly in the rhythms of her work today. But at the beginning of the fifties, after a visit to Europe, she turned to painting directly from nature. The light that transfuses her colour, and the daring spontaneity with which the pigment is handled, speak of her debt to French Impressionism as well as to newly found expressive depths within herself. When Nell Blaine feels a special empathy with her subject, as she does here, we too sense the participation of the artist: the 'breathing' rhythms of the paint transmitted in pure bright vibrant colours, evince her own vitality as well as that of her plants.

31
ALICE FORMAN
(American, *b.* 1931)

Madame Bovary's Shawl (1983)

Oil on canvas,
40 × 50 in. (101.6 × 127.1 cm.)
Collection of the artist

Alice Forman's paintings are far from being simply floral still lifes. Her wide reading, her dreams, her curiosity about past history and past owners, her strongly emotional response to flowers, all this is projected into her pictures which are documents of a rich inner life and of imaginative flights of fantasy.

The flowers that catch her attention are those that suggest unusual and telling relationships. The floppy yellow freesias holding sway in this particular picture, provide sprawling table company for the more politely compact African violets. In this context, botanical accuracy is of less concern to her than the expressive qualities of flowers, which really do seem to exude personalities of their own. The freesia, for example, possesses an almost playful animation in the way its head nods off the stem.

Alice Forman is very much alive to the correspondences between real flowers and the idealized flowers depicted on patterned fabrics. One day her daughter drew her attention to a softly coloured fringed shawl in an antique clothing shop called 'Madame Bovary'. Immediately it struck chromatic chords in Alice Forman's mind but the discovery also suggested certain social analogies with the pretentious Emma Bovary, echoes of which are suggested and lightly made fun of in the banquet-like setting of the table and its accessories. Alice Forman uses traditional still life subject matter to carry on a 'dialogue' with her environment sustained, as she describes it, 'in personal, poetic, and a painter's terms'. In this sense, *Madame Bovary's Shawl* might almost be termed a private conversation piece; the human presence is implied as much in the objects Alice Forman has selected as in the expressive touch of her brush, which fine-tunes edges and contours, and endows firm and fleshy surfaces with a richness that is at once sensuous and appealing. The conversation is about a season and Alice Forman's mood is buoyant: there is a sense of Spring in the air, vibrant with light and colour, after a dark winter.

32
FERNANDO BOTERO
(Colombian, *b.* 1932)

Florero (*Flowerpot*) (1970)

Oil on canvas,
75½ × 60½ in. (193 × 153·5 cm.)
Private collection

Fernando Botero painted a number of flower-pieces in the seventies, all of them featuring large bulbous vases piled high with flowers of every description—roses, dahlias, daisies, primroses as well as many fantasy flowers of the artist's own invention. They look as though each bloom has been pinned haphazardly onto a large mould, with tiny wild flowers tucked every which way into available spaces as a final decorative gesture. In another version of 1974, some of these smaller stems are already falling out, together with some stray petals. Only a society in which labour and flowers are cheap and abundant could afford such generous extravagance.

Botero has grown up with the daily sight of peasants carrying great baskets of flowers to market. He is as familiar with the huge paper flowers of Mexico as he is with daintily garlanded Madonnas and statues of Santa Rosa of Lima. His own home is decked out with lavish arrangements overflowing with fruit and flowers. But monumental and prodigal compositions like *Florero* exist only in his head. Later, in a very small preliminary sketch, they find their sculptural proportions and their carefully contrived design, frequently balanced by the miniature counterpoint of some tiny buzzing insect. But they are not painted in Latin America—this one was done in New York—and, like all his work, they owe as much to imagination as they do to local inspiration. Despite his academic self-training in Europe, the sources of his innocent vision and of his primitive shading and modelling lie in the Pre-Colombian and Colonial traditions of Latin America.

Botero now lives in Paris and he himself has admitted the effect of distance in inflating and distorting memory. Hence the larger than life Colombian primroses which sometimes appear in his bouquets. He has also explained that he inflates the appearance of familiar objects, almost overpowering us here with burgeoning flora, expressly to heighten our enjoyment.

GENERAL BOOKS FOR FURTHER REFERENCE

Apart from Blunt's survey, the following books all reproduce examples of contemporary flower painting:

ANDERSON, R. DENNIS *American Flower Painting* New York, 1980

BLUNT, WILFRED *The Art of Botanical Illustration* London, 1950 (an up-dated edition is in preparation)

FAHY, EVERETT *Metropolitan Flowers* New York: The Metropolitan Museum of Art, 1982

FOSHAY, ELLA M. *Reflections of Nature: Flowers in American Art* New York, in association with the Whitney Museum of American Art, 1984

HULTON, PAUL and LAWRENCE SMITH *Flowers in Art from East and West* London: British Museum Publications, 1979

KING, RONALD *Botanical Illustration* London, 1978

MITCHELL, PETER *European Flower Painters* London, 1973

WEST, KEITH *How to Draw Plants: The techniques of botanical illustration* London, in association with The British Museum (Natural History), 1983

ACKNOWLEDGMENTS

The author wishes to express grateful thanks to the artists concerned and to the following for valuable advice and information: Ella M. Foshay, Olda Kokoschka, Lucy Lim, Ishbel McWhirter, Catherine Martineau, Richard Morphet, Lady Ritchie of Dundee, James Sellars, Peyton Skipwith, Professor Michael Sullivan, Harry Torczyner and Tony Venison.

The publishers wish to make the following acknowledgements for copyrights and sources of illustrations: Marie Angel, © Marie Angel, 1980; Elizabeth Blackadder, Mercury Gallery, London; Nell Blaine, courtesy Fischbach Gallery, New York; Raymond Booth, The Fine Art Society, London; Fernando Botero, courtesy Marlborough Gallery, Inc., New York; Audrey Flack © DACS 1985, photo credit Dean Jacobson; Paul Gell, Francis Kyle Gallery, London; P. S. Gordon, courtesy Fischbach Gallery, New York; David Hockney, © David Hockney 1975; Oskar Kokoschka, © Cosmopress Geneva/ADAGP Paris 1986; Robert Kulicke, courtesy Davis and Langdale Company, New York; Joan Law-Smith, © Joan Law-Smith; Roy Lichtenstein, © DACS 1985; Magritte, © ADAGP 1986; Michael Mazur, courtesy Barbara Mathes Gallery, New York; Pat Steir, courtesy Michael Klein, Inc.; Pandora Sellars, courtesy of the British Museum (Natural History); Jean Marie Toulgouat, Francis Kyle Gallery, London; Paul Wonner, photography, courtesy Museum of Fine Arts, Boston; Robert Zakanitch, Robert Miller Gallery, New York; Georgia O'Keeffe photo by Malcolm Varon, NYC; Anne Marie Trechslin, © Anne Marie Trechslin.